I'M A GLOBAL CITIZEN

HUMAN RIGHTS

Written by Alice Harman

Illustrated by David Broadbent

W

Franklin Watts
First published in Great Britain in 2019 by The Watts Publishing Group
Copyright © The Watts Publishing Group, 2019

Produced for Franklin Watts by
White-Thomson Publishing Ltd
www.wtpub.co.uk

ISBN (HB): 978 1 4451 6403 8
ISBN (PB): 978 1 4451 6404 5

Series Editor: Georgia Amson-Bradshaw
Series Designer: David Broadbent
All Illustrations by: David Broadbent
Consultant: Dr Synne L. Dyvik

Printed in Dubai

Franklin Watts
An imprint of
Hachette Children's Group
Part of The Watts Publishing Group
Carmelite House
50 Victoria Embankment
London EC4Y 0DZ

An Hachette UK Company
www.hachette.co.uk
www.franklinwatts.co.uk

Facts, figures and dates were correct when going to press.

CONTENTS

Look out for this little book symbol to find definitions of important words. Other definitions can be found in the glossary on page 30.

What are human rights?

Our human rights are the basic rights and freedoms that belong to everyone. They are the basic needs for a healthy, safe life that allows us to all to reach our full potential.

Every single person has human rights from the moment they are born, no matter who they are. Nobody has to earn them and everyone's human rights are equal.

The government of a country is responsible for making sure that all its people have these rights.

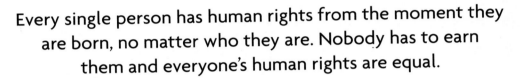

Living freely and well

Some human rights are to do with freedom – for example, our rights to live freely and not as a slave, to follow our religion and to have a family.

Others are about what we need in everyday life – for example, housing, healthcare, food and time to rest.

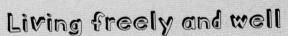

Looking out for everyone

Human rights aim to protect us from terrible things such as torture and abuse, and make sure we can leave places where we are in danger.

They also state that we should all be treated fairly and equally by the law, and should all have a say in how our country is run.

Your needs and rights

Think about the different needs you have in your everyday life – from basic things such as food and water to things like being listened to if you have a problem. Write down a list of all of them.

Ask a friend to do the same and compare your lists. Are there any differences?

What is the Universal Declaration of Human Rights?

The Universal Declaration of Human Rights is a document created by the United Nations (UN) in 1948. It gives a list of 30 rights that the UN believes every person in the world should have. It has been translated into more languages than any other text on Earth.

United Nations

An organisation of many different countries' governments that works for world peace, development and human rights.

Eleanor Roosevelt
USA

Alexander E. Bogomolov
USSR

John Peters Humphrey
Canada

Peng-chun Chang
China

Making history

The UN was formed in 1945, after the Second World War (1939–45) and the horrors of the Holocaust, to help work together to build a better, more peaceful world.

The Holocaust

The killing of millions of Jews and members of other groups by the Nazis during the Second World War.

Writing the Declaration

One of the UN's first tasks was to agree a list of human rights that everyone in the world should have, a standard for how every government should treat its people.

Over the next three years, the UN's member countries worked together to create the Universal Declaration of Human Rights. In 1948, members voted to accept it as a global standard of human rights.

Charles Dukes
UK

Hernán Santa Cruz
Chile

William Hodgson
Australia

Charles Habib Malik
Lebanon

René Cassin
France

A committee representing nine UN member countries produced the Universal Declaration of Human Rights, which 48 of the 58 countries in the UN voted to adopt.

The Declaration isn't a law, it is an ideal for countries to work towards. By agreeing to it, countries promise to try to make sure all their people have these rights. This often means that their national laws include at least some accepted human rights.

Turn to pages 28–29 to read a shortened, simplified version of the Declaration's 30 human rights.

Are human rights different for children?

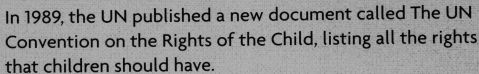

Children have the same human rights as adults, but there are some rights that don't apply until they have reached a certain age – for example, the right to get married.

Everyone under the age of 18 also has extra rights to keep them safe and give them the best chances for life. These weren't included in the Universal Declaration of Human Rights (see pages 6–7) but people later realised that children have needs that adults don't, such as the right to a safe, caring family.

Children's rights

In 1989, the UN published a new document called The UN Convention on the Rights of the Child, listing all the rights that children should have.

Which of the rights on the next page do you think are listed in the 1989 UN Convention on the Rights of the Child?

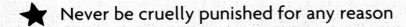

- ⭐ Never be cruelly punished for any reason

- ⭐ Be allowed time to play

- ⭐ Give your opinion and have adults take it seriously

- ⭐ Live in the same country as your parents

- ⭐ Choose your own friends

- ⭐ Only work if it is safe, you are paid and you can still go to school

- ⭐ Be protected from war, and not have to fight if you are under 15 years old.

- ⭐ Go to school and get a good education

- ⭐ Have access to information (for example, through books, radio and the internet)

- ⭐ Be given enough healthy food to eat

- ⭐ Choose a different religion to your parents, or no religion

Sorry, trick question! These are all rights that every child has, and their family and the government should make sure that they are respected. Many countries around the world have promised to make sure children have all these rights and more.

However, there is still far to go – for instance, today there are 152 million child workers around the world. In the poorest countries, one in four children has to work.

Why might people's human rights not be respected?

Sometimes people are treated in a way that doesn't seem to respect their human rights. You may have seen news stories or situations in your local community where this is the case.

Write down some examples, such as refugees not being helped to reach a safe place to live.

Refugee
A person forced to leave their country to escape danger and find safety in another place.

Poverty and war

It's a sad fact that in real life many people's human rights are not respected, for all sorts of complicated reasons. Perhaps a country is at war, so it's much more difficult for the government to make sure that everyone is safe and well.

Or a country might be very poor and not have enough money to help its people. Every year, millions of children die of preventable causes because they don't have good enough healthcare and living conditions.

Power and injustice

There can also be nastier reasons for human rights not being respected. We like to think the best of each other, but sometimes people behave cruelly, selfishly and unfairly towards others.

For example, a government might try to stay in power by stopping its people from criticising them, a business owner might use slaves or child labour to make more money, or a girl may be forced and threatened into child marriage because people don't think what she wants is important.

Look back at the examples of human rights issues that you wrote down at the start of page 10. What do you think the reasons might have been in each case for people's human rights not being respected?

What happens if human rights aren't respected?

What would you do if you saw a classmate at school being bullied? Hopefully, you would tell a teacher so that they can help protect them and stop the bullying. Your school has a responsibility to keep its students safe and able to focus on their education.

How governments can act

The government has a similar responsibility to protect the rights of everyone living in their country. The legal system – the police and the law courts – makes sure that people are punished for not respecting these rights.

However, people's human rights – and how well they are protected for everyone, not just certain people with more power and money – vary a lot from country to country.

How the UN can act

The UN documents that we've looked at (see pages 6–7 and 8–9) try to make these rights equal all over the world. But if a country doesn't respect the human rights listed in the documents, it's not technically breaking any law. However, the UN can still take action.

It has to use other methods to try to change things – for example, making the country look bad by talking publicly about what they are doing wrong. If this doesn't work, it can use sanctions, stop anyone selling the country weapons, or even vote to send in peacekeeping soldiers.

How you can act

If people in power – whether at a school or on a global scale – are not properly protecting people's rights, we can use our voices to try to make them. Protests, petitions, news stories, or even a simple letter of complaint, can let them know that people care and won't let them get away with it. You might be surprised at what a big impact you can make through these actions.

Sanctions
Non-violent penalties, such as banning trade with a country, that aim to change that country's actions.

Connected human rights

There are a lot of different human rights, and many of them connect up to each other. For example, if you are ill and your right to health care is not respected then you might not get better for a long time and you won't be able to go to school. This means you miss out on your right to education.

Think about these three scenarios and which human rights are not being respected in each one. Look at the full Universal Declaration of Human Rights on pages 28–29 to help you.

1. A young woman came to work as a live-in housekeeper for a family five years ago. Since then, she has not been paid and she is not allowed to leave the house. She has to sleep on the kitchen floor at night, she never has any time off, and she is pushed and shouted at if she ever accidentally drops something.

2. Two men are in love and want to get married. In their country, same-sex couples cannot get married, so they start an online campaign to change the law. Their posts are all deleted and their home address is posted online. They hold a meeting with other campaigners and the police burst in and arrest everyone there.

3. A boy wears a patka to school, as part of practising his Sikh religion and cultural heritage. He is sent home from school with a note for his parents saying that he is breaking the school dress code and must stop wearing the patka. The boy's teacher makes nasty jokes about him to the class and makes him sit under his desk if he talks back.

Patka
A small piece of cloth wrapped around the head.

15

Rights and restrictions

Our lives are hugely affected by whether or not our human rights are protected. We can either be helped to live a good, happy life or be unfairly forced to live in poor conditions and do things that make us unhappy.

Find two counters (two different coins work well) and a die, and play this game with a friend. Go up the ladders when your human rights are protected, and go down the snakes every time these rights are ignored.

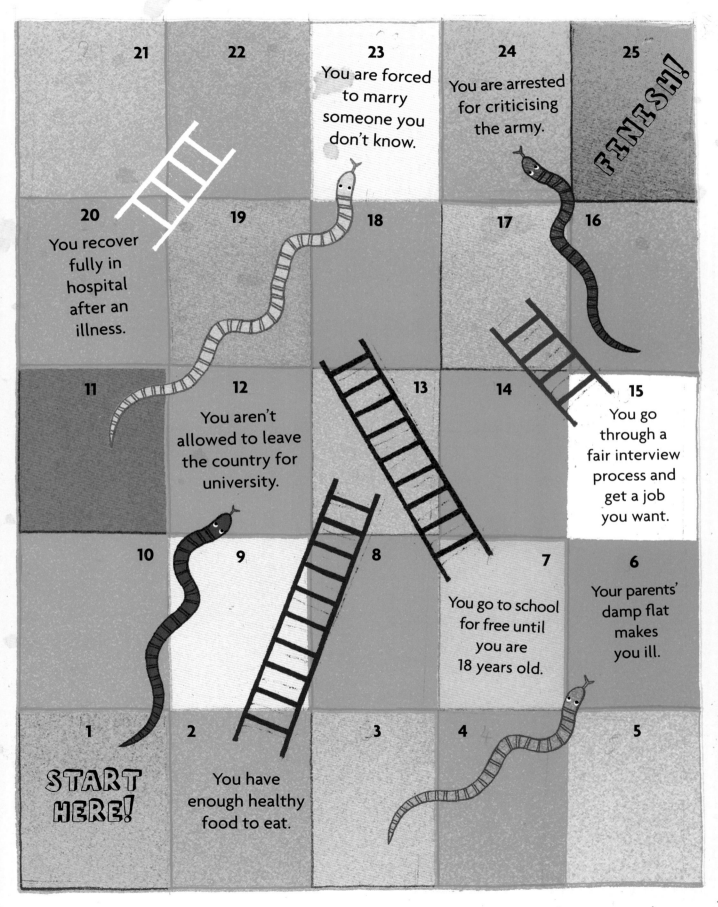

The limits of human rights

One of the most interesting questions about human rights is where to draw the line so that one person's rights do not take away the rights of another person. Some of our human rights have limits – for example, someone who is sent to prison for a violent attack has temporarily lost their right to freedom. This limit exists to respect their victim's right to personal safety and to similarly protect others from danger.

Other rights are absolute – in the same example, no matter what the person in prison has done they should never be tortured or killed. Some countries do have the death penalty for certain crimes, but this goes against the human rights set out by the UN.

Debate the following questions with a partner, tossing a coin to pick who will take which side. Remember that people often feel very differently about where the limits should be for certain rights.

1. A man becomes homeless and is given housing by the council several times but is removed each time, after several warnings, for abusing and threatening his neighbours. Is the council still responsible for housing him?

2. A group of friends and neighbours meets regularly to talk about how angry they are at non-white people moving to their area, and what they plan to do to stop it. These plans often involve violence and destruction of people's property. They have been meeting for six months and have not carried out an attack yet. Should they be allowed to meet?

3. A teacher has received a note saying that a girl at school is carrying a large knife in her bag and using it to threaten people into giving her money. The teacher asks to look in the girl's bag and she refuses. Would it be okay for the teacher to look in it anyway?

Making change happen: Black Lives Matter

Black Lives Matter is a global activist movement that aims to protect black people's human rights. It focuses particularly on black people's experiences of racism and violence from the police and of unfair treatment in the legal system.

Getting started

The movement began in the USA in 2013, when co-founders Alicia Garza, Patrisse Cullors and Opal Tometi created the hashtag #blacklivesmatter.

This was in response to the acquittal of George Zimmerman, a Hispanic-American man who confronted and killed Trayvon Martin, a 17-year-old African-American child, as Martin was innocently walking home from the local shop.

Acquittal
When someone is found not guilty of a crime at court.

Hispanic
Someone whose ancestors are from a Spanish-speaking country in North, Central or South America.

A growing movement

The online campaign grew and grew through 2013 and 2014. In August 2014, members organised the first in-person Black Lives Matter national protest, with around 500 people taking part. They joined other groups protesting in Ferguson, USA, after the police killed an unarmed black 18-year-old called Michael Brown.

Black Lives Matter has since grown into a global network and its members have staged thousands of protests around the world.

Impact and influence

Black Lives Matter has helped many people understand how racist attitudes can take away people's human rights – or even their lives.

It is tricky to measure the impact of a new, ongoing movement such as Black Lives Matter, as changes in the law and society can take a long time. What it has done is increase public attention and pressure on people in power to make those changes.

Just as importantly, it has also encouraged a new generation of activists to fight for their human rights.

Profile: Kailash Satyarthi

When Kailash Satyarthi was a young boy of five, growing up in India, he saw a boy his age mending shoes on the street outside the school. When he asked adults why the boy wasn't in school like him, he was told that the boy's family was poor and so he had to work instead.

Kailash was horrified at how the adults just accepted this unfair situation for children. From the age of 11, Kailash raised money to pay poor children's school fees and collected thousands of donated school books for them to use.

Kailash studied to be an electrical engineer but never forgot his true calling to fight for children's rights. At 26 years old, he left behind his well-paid career to found Bachpan Bachao Andolan, the Save Childhood Movement.

Since 1980, this organisation has freed 83,000 children from slave-like working conditions and given them the education they were denied.

In 1994, Kailash set up an organisation called Rugmark (now called GoodWeave International) to help end illegal child labour in the rug-making industry. GoodWeave gives out a special logo, and if shoppers see it on a rug they know no child labour was used to make it.

In 1998, Kailash led the Global March against Child Labour – an 80,000 km march across 103 countries to demand an end to this practice around the world. This protest helped to change the law in over 150 countries to make the worst, most dangerous forms of child labour illegal.

Kailash has since led many high-profile children's rights and education campaigns in India and internationally, often through his own foundation. He won the Nobel Peace Prize in 2014, along with Malala Yousafzai, and he has received many other awards and honours. His work continues to this day.

Activate!
Make a human rights wall

One of the most important things you can do to fight for human rights is to spread awareness to others and inspire them to take action. Why not try making a human rights wall to do just that?

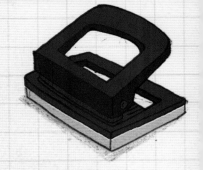

1. Hand out a sheet of A4 paper to everyone in your class, with a hole punched in each corner of the paper.

2. Ask the class to talk in groups about what human rights are, and to think about some of the freedoms and rights in their life that are most important to them.

3. Now ask everyone to think of a realistic action that they can take to support human rights. Here are some ideas: writing to someone in government about an issue you care about, donating to a local food bank, raising money for an education charity.

4. Ask everyone to write or draw a promise to complete their chosen action on their sheet of paper, and decorate it. They can work together in pairs or small groups on bigger actions that take a longer time.

5. Spread out all of the finished promise sheets, and thread long pieces of string down through the holes on either side, knotting them at the bottom. Then tie short pieces of string around each of the vertical strings, to make one big wall hanging. Ask a teacher to help you hang it somewhere in the school where everyone will see it.

6. Next term, bring the wall hanging back into class and ask everyone to give an update on what action they took, how they felt and what results they saw. You could even have everyone write their update on the back of their promise sheet.

organise! A human rights rally

Hold a human rights rally to help people understand how important human rights are and what they can do to help protect them.

Split a big group of your friends or classmates into small groups. Each group decides which cause they want to support – anything from standing up for disabled people's rights to welcoming refugees into your country.

Rally

A group meeting where people protest or show their support for a cause.

The group then does some research into their chosen issue and decides what sort of activity they want to hold on the day. Here are a few activity ideas to get you started.

Change is possible

Make a display about positive changes in human rights in recent years — for instance, women in Saudi Arabia campaigned bravely and finally won the right to vote in 2015.

Stage a protest

Make colourful banners and signs about your issue, then lead a march around the rally holding them in the air. Try to get some good photos and video!

In their shoes

Create a short interactive play where the audience is shown what it would be like to experience your chosen issue. For example, they could take the part of a group of girls who are not allowed to go to school.

Spread the word

Make and show a short video about a human rights issue that may not be well known. For instance, do some research into countries where people still cannot vote freely for their government. Try some different, creative techniques to make your point.

Universal Declaration of Human Rights

These are shortened and simplified versions of the 30 human rights included in the UN Declaration of Human Rights (see pages 6–7). To read them in full, visit un.org/en/universal-declaration-human-rights

We all have the right to:

1. Be treated equally to other people

2. Not be treated unfairly because of race, gender or any other reason

3. Life, freedom and personal safety

4. Not be kept in slavery

5. Not be tortured or cruelly punished

6. Be recognised as a person by the legal system

7. Be treated equally in the legal system

8. Legal justice when our rights are not respected

9. Not be arrested, held or sent abroad without good reason

10. A fair, public legal process if we are accused of crimes

11. Be considered innocent until proven guilty

12. Privacy for ourselves and our family

13. Move freely within our own country and leave any country

14. Come to a new country to escape danger and unfair treatment

15. Have a nationality and change it if wanted

16. Choose freely to marry and have a family

17. Own property and not have it taken away for no reason

18. Hold and follow our beliefs and religion

19. Hold and express our opinions and exchange information

20. Freely meet with others for peaceful reasons

21. Vote freely, take part in government and access public services

22. Necessary support if unemployed, disabled, ill or elderly

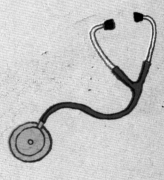

23. Choose our own work and be treated fairly and equally

24. Rest and leisure time

25. A decent living standard, including housing, food and health care

26. Education, including at least early education for free

27. Participate in community life and enjoy arts and sciences

28. A level of social order that makes all these human rights possible

29. Fulfil our responsibilities, respecting others and their rights

30. Not have any of these human rights taken away or disrespected

Glossary

activism promoting a cause and working for social change

acquittal when someone is found not guilty of a crime at court

gender how a person sees their identity as a woman or a man, or both or neither – it doesn't always match up with the sex (girl, boy or intersex) they were given at birth

heritage something that is handed down from the past and is part of your culture and background

Hispanic someone whose ancestors are from a Spanish-speaking country in North, Central or South America

Holocaust, the the killing of millions of Jews and members of other groups by the Nazis during the Second World War

human rights things that everyone must be allowed, no matter what country they live in – for example, the right to education and to be treated equally by the law

nationality describes the country in which you were born, or to which you moved to and became and legal citizen - for example, someone born in France is of French nationality

patka a short piece of cloth wrapped around the head, often worn by boys following the religion of Sikhism

petition a written document, often signed by lots of people, asking someone with power to do or change something

race a group of people who share some of the same physical features, such as skin colour

rally a group meeting where people protest or show their support for a cause

refugee a person forced to leave their country to escape danger and find safety in another place

sanctions penalties that don't use violence, such as banning trade with a country, that aim to change that country's actions

slavery people owning other people, or making them work without pay and stopping them from living freely

torture deliberately causing someone a huge amount of physical or emotional pain

United Nations an organisation of many countries' governments that works for world peace, development and human rights

Universal Declaration of Human Rights an international document that lists and describes the rights that everyone in the world should have

Further information

Who Are Refugees and Migrants? What Makes People Leave Their Homes? and other Big Questions by Michael Rosen and Annemarie Young (Wayland, 2016)
In this book you can discover the history of migration around the world and issues today. Learn more about diversity, multiculturalism and the prejudice and discrimination that people can face.

***Brilliant Women: Heroic Leaders and Activists* by Georgia Amson-Bradshaw (Wayland, 2018)**
Meet women through history who have fought for change and human rights. Read their stories, then complete fun activities to help you become a great, world-changing activist too!

***Putting Peace First: 7 Commitments to Change the World* by Eric David Dawson (Viking, 2018)**
When he was just 18 years old, Eric David Dawson co-founded the non-profit Peace First based on the idea that young people can change the world for the better – not someday, but right now. This handbook helps you to do just that, with inspiring stories and step-by-step explanations of how activists and peacemakers achieved their goals.

Websites

amnesty.org.uk/what-amnesty-youth-group
Watch the inspiring video on this page about a group of students at a London school campaigning to stop a woman in Iran, Sakineh Mohammadi Ashtiani, from receiving the death penalty. Sakineh was freed two years later, at least partly thanks to international protests like this one.

Amnesty International is a global organisation that campaigns to end abuses of human rights around the world. Learn more about joining or setting up an Amnesty youth group, as these students did. Work with others to campaign for human rights issues that really matter to you.

youtube.com/watch?v=TFMqTDIYI2U
This video looks in detail at children's rights and how the UN works to make sure countries uphold them. It has a lot of useful information but some of the words and ideas might not be familiar to you, so try watching it a couple of times through to make sure that it makes sense.

youtube.com/watch?v=_OUpsWCvE38&t=11s
A short video imagining the refugee crisis from another perspective. What if it was families from western Europe travelling and trying to reach safety in Africa?

malala.org/malalas-story
Learn about Malala Yousafzai, a campaigner for every girl's right to education and a life free from gender discrimination. She survived being shot in the head at the age of fifteen because of her activism, going on to win the Nobel Peace Prize and continue to inspire people around the world.

Note to parents and teachers: every effort has been made by the Publishers to ensure websites are suitable for children, that they are of the highest educational value, and that they contain no inappropriate or offensive material. However, because of the nature of the Internet, it is impossible to guarantee that the contents of these sites will not be altered. We strongly advise that Internet access is supervised by a responsible adult.

Index